The Flag

by Cameron Grieft
illustrated by George Ulrich

Practice Decodable 2

I0805997

McGraw Hill Education

Bothell, WA • Chicago, IL • Columbus, OH • New York, NY

MHEonline.com

Send all inquiries to:
McGraw-Hill Education
8787 Orion Place
Columbus, OH 43240

ISBN: 978-0-02-140713-2
MHID: 0-02-140713-4

Printed in the United States of America.

7 8 9 CTM 23

Is the  up?

sun

The  is up.

sun

See the  .

school

Is the  up?

flag

See the  .

flag

The  is up.

flag